The U.S. Armed Forces

The U.S. Army Golden Knights

by Carrie A. Braulick

Consultant:
Barbara J. Fox
Reading Specialist
North Carolina State University

Capstone
press

Mankato, Minnesota

Blazers is published by Capstone Press,
151 Good Counsel Drive, P.O. Box 669, Mankato, Minnesota 56002.
www.capstonepress.com

Library of Congress Cataloging-in-Publication Data
Braulick, Carrie A., 1975–
    The U.S. Army Golden Knights / by Carrie A. Braulick.
    p. cm.—(Blazers. The U.S. Armed Forces)
    Summary: "Describes the U.S. Army Golden Knights, including
their formations and maneuvers, planes, equipment, and team member
duties"—Provided by publisher.
    Includes bibliographical references and index.
    ISBN 0-7368-4393-0 (hardcover)
    1. United States. Army. Parachute Team—Juvenile literature. 2. Parachuting—
United States—Juvenile literature. 3. Skydiving—United States—Juvenile literature.
I. Title. II. Series.
UD483.B743 2006
797.5'6'0973—dc22   2004027805

Credits
Juliette Peters, set designer; Patrick D. Dentinger, book designer; Jo Miller, photo
    researcher; Scott Thoms, photo editor

Photo Credits
DVIC/Allan Harding, 27; Don S. Montgomery, USN, 8
The Image Finders/T. A. Wagner Photo, 15
Photo courtesy of U.S. Army/Spc. Bill Putnam, 26
Unicorn Stock Photos/Dennis Thompson, 19; Jay Foreman, 25; Michael Massey,
    18; Terry Barner, 9
USAPT, Media Relations Office, cover (both), 5, 6, 11, 12, 13, 14, 17, 21,
    22–23, 28–29

**Capstone Press thanks Donna Council, media relations director,
U.S. Army Golden Knights, for her assistance in preparing this book.**

1 2 3 4 5 6 10 09 08 07 06 05

Table of Contents

The Golden Knights in Action 4

Maneuvers 10

Planes and Equipment 16

Golden Knight Jobs 24

Golden Knight Equipment 22

Glossary 30

Read More 31

Internet Sites 31

Index 32

The Golden Knights in Action

Golden Knights jump out of a plane. They speed toward the ground. A large crowd watches them from below.

Bomb burst

The Golden Knights latch onto one another. They make the bomb burst formation. Smoke rises from their feet.

BLAZER FACT

Jumpers can reach speeds of 100 miles (160 kilometers) per hour before opening their parachutes.

Seconds later, the jumpers' parachutes pop open. The Golden Knights float safely to the ground.

Maneuvers

The U.S. Army Golden Knights formed in 1959. Their parachuting maneuvers have made them famous.

In free-fall maneuvers, jumpers make formations before opening their parachutes. The Golden Knights' free-fall competition team has won many awards.

For other maneuvers, jumpers
open their parachutes. Sometimes, they
line up their parachutes side by side.
They also hook together to make stacks.

Planes and Equipment

Golden Knights often jump out of C-31A Troopship planes. These large planes were made to carry troops and supplies.

Smoke canisters attach to jumpers' heels. The smoke makes colorful patterns in the sky.

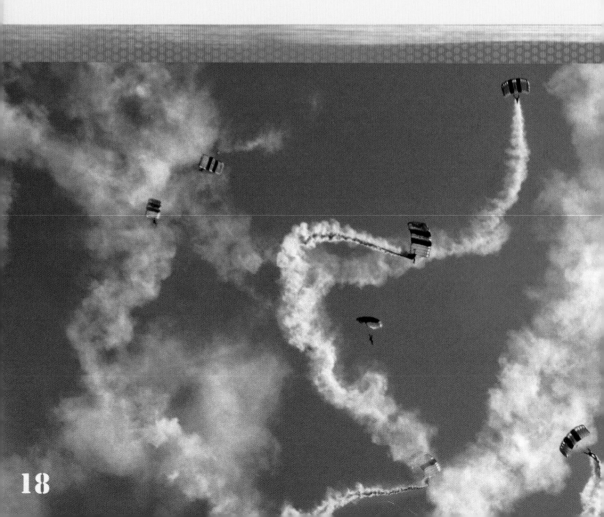

BLAZER FACT

Golden Knights do not always perform maneuvers. In accuracy competitions, they try to land in the center of a landing pad.

Jumpers have a reserve parachute to use if the main one doesn't open. Helmets and goggles also protect jumpers.

Parachute pack

Helmet

Goggles

Golden Knight
Equipment

Boots

Helmet

Gloves

Goggles

Smoke canister

Parachute pack

Jumpsuit

23

Golden Knight Jobs

Golden Knights don't just perform at shows. They also pack parachutes, fly planes, and plan shows.

Golden Knights teach their skills to others. They spend a lot of time practicing for their shows. Their exciting moves keep crowds coming to see them year after year.

BLAZER FACT

The Golden Knights sometimes walk through their maneuvers on the ground before doing them in the air.

Golden Knights
in a stack

Glossary

canister (KAN-uh-stur)—a rounded container

formation (for-MAY-shuhn)—a pattern or shape formed by a group of parachute jumpers

goggles (GOG-uhlz)—glasses that fit tightly around the eyes to protect them

helmet (HEL-mit)—a hard hat that protects the head

maneuver (muh-NOO-ver)—a planned and controlled movement

parachute (PA-ruh-shoot)—a large piece of strong, lightweight fabric; parachutes allow people to jump from high places and float slowly and safely to the ground.

Read More

Cooper, Jason. *U.S. Army.* Fighting Forces. Vero Beach, Fla.: Rourke, 2004.

Hopkins, Ellen. *Air Devils: Sky Racers, Sky Divers, and Stunt Pilots.* Cover-to-Cover Books. Logan, Iowa: Perfection Learning, 2000.

Hopkins, Ellen. *The Golden Knights: The U.S. Army Parachute Team.* Serving Your Country. Mankato, Minn.: Capstone Press, 2001.

Internet Sites

FactHound offers a safe, fun way to find Internet sites related to this book. All of the sites on FactHound have been researched by our staff.

Here's how:

1. Visit *www.facthound.com*
2. Type in this special code **0736843930** for age-appropriate sites. Or enter a search word related to this book for a more general search.
3. Click on the **Fetch It** button.

FactHound will fetch the best sites for you!

Index

bomb burst, 7

competitions, 12, 13, 19

goggles, 20

helmets, 20

maneuvers, 7, 10, 12, 14,
    19, 27
    free-fall, 7, 12
    stacks, 14

parachutes, 7, 8, 12, 14,
    20, 24
planes, 4, 16, 24

smoke, 7, 18
smoke canisters, 18

training, 27